STATIONS OF THE CROSS

STATIONS OF THE CROSS

Timothy Radcliffe

Art by Martin Erspamer

LITURGICAL PRESS
Collegeville, Minnesota

www.litpress.org

Cover design Ann Blattner.

Stations of the Cross art by Martin Erspamer, OSB, a monk of Saint Meinrad Archabbey.

1	2	3	4	5	6	7	8	9

Library of Congress Control Number: 2014943930

ISBN 978-0-8146-4953-4 978-0-8146-4978-7 (ebook)

CONTENTS

PREFACE

Almost every Catholic church has the Stations of the Cross on its walls. Moving from each station to the next, we accompany Jesus on his short journey from the palace of Pontius Pilate in Jerusalem, where he was condemned to death, to the cross and then to his tomb. This brief and tortuous journey happened in a hot and dusty city in the Middle East two thousand years ago. What sense does it make to reenact it in churches from Alaska to Cape Town today? What is going on?

This ancient devotion is the fruit of two traditions that are in fruitful tension with each other. On the one hand, God is everywhere; we do not have to go to any special place to encounter the divine. God is just as much in Johannesburg or Jakarta as Jerusalem. On the other hand, God became flesh and blood in this particular human being, who lived in a remote outpost of the Roman Empire, which therefore remains for us still today the Holy Land. We ignite interesting insights when contrasting traditions rub against each other!

The Christians of the first century believed strongly in God's omnipresence. We do not need holy places to be in contact with God. Jesus said to the Samaritan woman at the well, "believe me, the hour is coming when neither on this mountain nor in Jerusalem will you worship the Father" (John 4:21). Stephen, the first martyr, is arrested because he "never ceases to speak words against this holy place" (Acts 6:13), the temple. The expansion of Christianity around the Mediterranean and the destruction of the temple in AD 70 confirmed this new faith in its liberation from any holy places. You can be a Christian anywhere.

Christianity had globalization in its DNA from the beginning! Gregory of Nyssa in the fourth century claimed "a change of place does not bring one closer to God, but there where you are God will come toward you." Martin Luther scorned Christians who venerated holy places: "As for the tomb in which the Lord lay, which the Saracens now possess, God values it like all the cow pastures in Switzerland."

But from the beginning, this was in tension with another tradition, which tapped into the universal religious desire to go on pilgrimage. Christianity kept alive the Jewish love for Jerusalem and the temple. "The Lord loves the gates of Zion / more than all the dwelling places of Jacob" (Ps 87:2). It has been claimed that the passion narrative in Mark's gospel is rooted in the earliest version of the Stations of the Cross, as pilgrims followed the route of Jesus' last hours (Rowan Williams, *Meeting God in Mark*). The angel says to the women at the empty tomb, "see the place where they laid him" (Mark 16:6). From the very beginning people did indeed come to see.

The cult of the martyrs led to pilgrimages to their tombs. From the fourth century onward, the Holy Land became the archetypal goal of pilgrims. Constantine's mother, Helena, claimed to have found there the true cross and the tomb of Jesus. Pilgrims came to see the places where Jesus had lived and died. Saint Jerome wrote to Marcella, "Each time that we enter the tomb, we see the Saviour lying on his winding sheet: if we stop there for just a moment we can still see the angel seated at his feet and at his head the folded shroud."

But most Christians from Western Europe could never make their way to Jerusalem. It was too far, too expensive, and extremely dangerous, especially in times of conflict between Christianity and Islam. The Stations of the Cross evolved so that anyone anywhere could make that pilgrimage without leaving home. You just had to go to your local church. It was a brilliant reconciliation of those conflicting convictions, each of which cherishes a truth of our faith: God is everywhere, and it is wonderful that he shared our lives at a particular time and place. Anywhere in the world, from Chicago to Tokyo, you can walk with Jesus, see him embrace his mother and meet the daughters of Jerusalem, be crucified and buried.

This is a beautiful expression of the core of our faith, which is that Jesus embraced the dramas of every human life, our triumphs and failures, our joys and sorrows. In the Stations of the Cross, we remember how the Lord is with us, especially when we seem to be stuck and have lost the way forward. He walks with us, and trips with us when we stumble and helps us to our feet again.

It all begins with his condemnation to death. This is when he enters into his passion. It is not just that he suffers; that had begun long before. "Passion" literally means that things are done to him. He is treated as an object. He is condemned; he is made to carry a cross; he is overcome by exhaustion; he is nailed, pierced, killed, and buried. He is with us every time we feel that our lives are not in our own hands, when we feel pushed around, subjected to humiliation, victimized and used, drifting helpless toward our death.

Each station recalls a moment when Jesus stopped. A "station" means simply a place of stopping, as trains stop in railway stations. He stops to talk to people in compassion; he stops when he falls to the ground out of exhaustion, unable to carry on; he stops at Golgotha because that is the end of the road. Jesus is close to us when we too are stopped in our tracks and wonder whether we can carry on anymore. We may be halted by illness or failure, by grief or despair. But Jesus carries on, making his slow way to the cross and to the resurrection, and brings us with himself in hope. Let us set out.

JESUS IS CONDEMNED TO DEATH

Jesus' trial is a farce. Pontius Pilate does not think that he is guilty. He washes his hands of any guilt, but he makes little effort to save Jesus. Is this because he is a weary cynic who does not care? "What is truth?" he asks Jesus (John 18:38). Or is it because it is good to look tough on crime, even if the wrong person gets the punishment? Maybe he is just afraid of Jesus' accusers. So, after a token resistance, he goes with the crowd.

All over the world people are facing execution for similar reasons. Sister Helen Prejean showed in *Dead Man Walking* that many people, especially poor black people in the United States, are sentenced to death without a proper defense because the lawyers have not studied the case and appear not to care. Still today governors do not want to look soft and risk unpopularity.

So innocent people go to their death. Think of the one hundred thousand Christians who die every year just because of their faith. They share the condemnation of our Lord.

But don't we often do the same thing, condemning people without much attention to what they really think and do? Poor people are judged to be scroungers, lazy, and feckless. We are quick to judge others. Maybe this is because we fear to stand out from the crowd. It is dangerous to disagree with the majority.

Sometimes we just cannot be bothered to discover the truth. I was sitting next to a lay university chaplain at lunch who dismissed with contempt a document prepared by the bishops of England and Wales. I said, "But it is a beautiful and nuanced document." She replied, "I do not do nuance." Truth and justice demand nuance, patiently teasing out the truth before we say anything.

Jesus is accused by his enemies. He bears all the accusations that we load on the backs of others, all the malicious words of condemnation and denigration. Our media are filled with accusation and contempt. We make other people the butt of jokes and ridicule. When we do that, Jesus bears it. But when he comes to judge us on the last day, he will judge us with kindness, with forgiveness. We have condemned him every time we have scorned and despised people, but he will let us go free if we but say yes to his mercy.

Jesus is condemned to death. He takes upon himself the sentence that we all face. The one thing of which we are sure is that one day we shall die. We all know our birthdays. We also have death days, the annual day of our coming death, but we do not know which day it is. People who are dying often have an acute sense of the gift of being still alive. If we remember that we too are condemned to die, then we may live every day as precious and unrepeatable, with the gifts and graces the Lord will give us today. Lord, give us gratitude for this day, and every day until we die.

Second Station

JESUS RECEIVES THE CROSS

What a humiliation to be forced to carry the instrument of his own death! It is like the Jews during the Holocaust who were made to dig their own graves. This was the crossbeam that will be raised up on the vertical pole of the cross. It must have been heavy if it was to bear his weight. He bears the weight of everything that we have laid on other people.

Just think of the burdens we have laid on those who love us. At times we may have placed heavy weights on our parents, for example, when we failed to show them love, or repaid a smile with a cross word. We were all once sulky teenagers! Think of the loads we have placed on our husbands or wives, when a kind glance or word could have eased them. Have we relieved people who came to us weighed down, looking for consolation and reassurance? Maybe we have been like the scribes and Pharisees, who "bind heavy burdens, hard to bear, and lay them on [people's] shoulders; but they themselves will not move them with their finger" (Matt 23:4).

But Jesus lifts these burdens onto his back, as God lifted the weight of slavery off the Israelites in Egypt and set them free. Jesus says to us, "Come to me, all who labor and are heavy laden, and I will give you rest. Take my yoke upon you, . . . and you will find rest for your souls" (Matt 11:28-29). His yoke is easy because he is yoked to us, and carries the strain of it.

In the Middle Ages Satan was always portrayed as serious, ponderous, noting down all our failures, loading them on our backs, the Great Accountant. Jesus bears the weight so that we may be liberated from a terrible seriousness and know spontaneous joy. Those who believe that Jesus carries our burdens know that we need not take ourselves too seriously! So we may walk with a light step and be carefree. May we "bear one another's burdens, and so fulfil the law of Christ" (Gal 6:2).

Jesus says that if we are to be his disciples, then we must take up our cross and follow him. That may sound rather masochistic, as if we must positively want to suffer. Sometimes it has made Christianity seem grim. But it means that we dare to embrace the life that is given to us, with its joys and suffering, its blessings and limitations. It is no good wishing that we were someone else. This is our life, a gift from God, and even its rough and hard moments are steps toward happiness.

The father of my closest friend at school had been a pilot in the RAF in the Second World War. He was shot down and badly burnt. His face was scarred and most of his fingers burnt off. I was afraid to meet him, but he bore his affliction with such courage and joy that after two minutes I never thought of it again. He became almost a second father to me. He had always wanted to be a teacher, but it was hard to get a job because of his disfigurement. And so he bought a school and became a brilliant and much-loved teacher and headmaster. He picked up his cross and seemed to carry it lightly. May we walk lightly too.

Third Station

JESUS FALLS
FOR THE FIRST TIME

W e all have many "first falls." There is the first time that we consciously disobey our parents, the first lie, the first sexual misdemeanour. We get married and think that we shall live in perfect bliss forever, and then there is the first quarrel, or maybe the first betrayal of some sort. When I became a Dominican I imagined that a life of unsullied holiness stretched ahead, but I had my first fall! If we become parents there will be other first falls, when we suddenly realize to our shame that we have been harsh to the child whom we love beyond words. Priests will have their first fall after ordination.

First falls are marked by shame and denial. They shake our self-image. After eating of the fruit, Adam blames it on Eve: "The woman whom [you gave] to be with me, she gave me fruit of the tree, and I ate"

(Gen 3:12). Eve also passes the buck: "The serpent beguiled me, and I ate" (v. 13). So it is God's fault, or that of the other person or the serpent. But it cannot be me. I am not like that. I am not the sort of person who would betray my marriage or the sort of priest who would betray his vocation.

We may be tempted to blame it on someone else, or on having had too much to drink, or because we were tired or depressed. Then let us remember that Jesus is close to us and has borne the shame of all first fallers and continues to do so.

We can then dare to look at ourselves with honesty, and know that we are indeed just that sort of person. We are not the perfect parents, or the amazing spouses, or the spotless pious priests that we may have imagined. But God smiles on us as we are, warts and all. We may not be perfect but neither are we despicable worms. We are fallible human beings who fumble our way to the kingdom, keeling over from time to time. Pope Francis wrote in *Evangelii Gaudium*, "Appearances notwithstanding, every person is immensely holy and deserves our love" (274). We dare to look at the people who seem so awful to us, rid our faces of judgmental frowns, and glimpse their goodness too.

Fourth Station

JESUS IS MET
BY HIS BLESSED MOTHER

Mary is there at the beginning. She is center stage at the annunciation; she presents her child in the temple, and raises him; she is there at the marriage feast in Cana. And then she falls into the background as the new community of disciples is born. Jesus says, "Here are my mother and my brothers! Whoever does the will of God is my brother, and sister, and mother" (Mark 3:34-35). She is invisible in the crowd.

Mothers and, indeed, fathers love their children by giving them space and getting out of the way. Parents encourage their children to make friends at school, become infatuated with boyfriends and girlfriends, live their own lives. One day the children leave the nest and make their homes with others who have become the center of their lives. But parents remain there if things collapse. My mother said she thought that her role as a mother would finish when her youngest child left home, but she discovered that one never ceases to be a mother. When I was master of the Dominicans, frequently changing planes at Heathrow Airport, my mother's house nearby became a refuge where I could get over jet lag. I needed her care all over again!

There is no bond so deep as that which binds a mother to her child. The Hebrew word for mercy is derived from the word for womb. Mothers are bound to their children by an umbilical cord of compassion. The poet Robert Burns wrote,

> The mother-linnet in the brake
> Bewails her ravish'd young;
> So I, for my lost darling's sake,
> Lament the live-day long.

Fathers feel this deep bond in their way too. King David is crushed by the death of the son who rebelled against him: "O my son Absalom, my son, my son Absalom! Would I had died instead of you, O Absalom, my son, my son!" (2 Sam 18:33).

Think of the compassion with which we look at our own parents, when we register for the first time that they are not semi-divine beings but fragile mortal people, just like ourselves. Seamus Heaney remembers seeing his father in all his vulnerability after an accident:

> I saw him face to face, he came to me
> With his damp footprints out of the river,
> And there was nothing between us there
> That might not still be happily ever after.

The utter selflessness of Mary and Jesus must have made each acutely aware of the suffering of the other. Did this make the pain more terrible, or was it eased because it was shared?

The death of a child before his or her parents is outrageous. It contradicts the natural order of things. It is the child who ought to care for parents and bury them. This is what Pope John Paul II called the "'covenant' between generations" (*Evangelium Vitae* 94). This is the appalling suffering of parents who lose their children in war or to illness. Mrs. Margaret Smith, from the north of England, lost five of her six sons in the First World War. She used to say, "Don't have boys. They just grow up to be cannon fodder." Think of the mothers whose children disappeared during the years of dictatorship in Argentina, Las Madres de Plaza de Mayo, who did not even have the bodies of their children to bury. As the ghost of the captain says in the film *Gravity*, "Your kid died. Doesn't get any rougher than that."

All this scandalous suffering is embraced by God when Jesus and his mother meet on the way to the cross. "As one whom his mother comforts, / so I will comfort you; / you shall be comforted in Jerusalem" (Isa 66:13). Jesus is every child lost prematurely, and Mary is every parent grieving for his or her child.

Fifth Station

SIMON OF CYRENE HELPS JESUS TO CARRY HIS CROSS

After a moment of great tenderness, the meeting of a mother and her child, there is as different an encounter as one could imagine, of two strangers whose lives briefly intersect. What might it have meant for each?

Jesus told his disciples that each must carry his own cross. Now he finds that he can no longer carry his own. He needs help. Maybe the soldiers are hustling him onward because they want to get this gruesome duty over as quickly as possible so that they can have a drink with their friends. According to the timing of John's gospel, the Sabbath is drawing near, and so everything must be over and done with before it begins (John 19:31). This slow stumbling man has become an inconvenience. So Simon of Cyrene is compelled to help. Surely this was not out of compassion for Jesus, just impatience to get a gruesome task over and done with.

Western culture has promoted the ideal of the self-sufficient person who does not need anyone else. We should stand on our own feet. It is humiliating to need others, especially strangers. When I had an operation on my back, I needed strangers to keep me clean, turn me over in bed, get me out of bed, and walk me to the lavatory. But this dependency is part of being human, and is embraced by God in Jesus at this moment. God says to St. Catherine of Siena, "I could well have supplied each of you with all your needs, both spiritual and material. But I wanted to make you dependent on one another so that each of you would be my minister, dispensing the graces and gifts you have received from me." In Jesus, we see God needing us, needing a drink from the Samaritan woman at the well, needing help with carrying his cross. It's okay to be needy.

Simon of Cyrene seems to have been just passing by when he got caught up in the drama of this man whom he probably did not even know. He had no choice. And yet Mark gives us the impression that he became a disciple whose children, Alexander and Rufus, were known to the community. Surely it must have been this involuntary encounter that changed his life. Having been forced to carry this stranger's cross, he became his disciple.

Suffering may come across us suddenly. Life is fine, we are happy, and then unexpectedly we have an accident, or discover an illness, or become unemployed. We may cry out, "It's unfair! Why me? Why now?" We may be constrained to carry the cross when we least expect it. May it be for us too a moment of grace, when we discover a new intimacy with the Lord, sharing his burden. As Paul wrote, "Now I rejoice in my sufferings for your sake, and in my flesh I complete what is lacking in Christ's afflictions for the sake of his body, that is, the church, of which I became a minister" (Col 1:24).

Sixth Station

VERONICA WIPES
THE FACE OF JESUS

There is a legend that on his way to the cross, a woman takes pity on Jesus and wipes his face. The image of his face is left imprinted on the towel. Hence her name, Veronica, which means "the true image."

The story is not found before the thirteenth century, but it embodies a deep truth. Israel longed to be blessed by seeing the face of God: "How long, O LORD? [Will you] forget me for ever? / How long [will you] hide [your] face from me?" (Ps 13:1). The face of God became flesh in the face of Jesus, who smiled upon sinners with tenderness. He looked with pleasure on pompous little Zacchaeus up in the tree and decided to stay with him rather than the self-righteous and respectable people. He smiled on Levi, another tax collector, and called him to discipleship. He looked with kindness on Peter after he had betrayed him.

But what about us? We do not see his face and we do not even know what Jesus looked like. We are the Body of Christ and so we must be his face. In Graham Greene's *Monsignor Quixote*, the priest calls the human face "the mirror image of God." We are smiled upon by the invisible God, and this is mirrored in our faces. As children we learn to smile by being smiled at by our parents and others. We gather around babies, and make funny noises, and smile. We learn a gaze filled with grace from the gracious smile with which God looks at us. Pope Francis said, "Here, this is me, a sinner on whom the Lord has turned his gaze." He reflects that smile in turn on the crowds around him.

Faces can crush people. Havana and Baghdad were dominated by the overbearing faces of Fidel Castro and Saddam Hussein. The police and immigration officers in many countries intimidate. The poor become accustomed to being frowned on. More than half of people today live in cities, often starved of faces that offer recognition. The people whom you see in today's vast urban deserts have faces that are usually frozen, unseeing. Visual contact is avoided out of fear or indifference.

The old pastor in Marilynne Robinson's *Gilead* says, "Any human face is a claim on you, because you can't help but understand the singularity of it, the courage and loneliness of it." It belongs to the ministry of every baptized person to be the face of Christ in the ordinary interactions of our daily lives. It is the small but necessary beginning of all Christian witness. According to the legend, Jesus on the way to the cross found among a crowd of hostile faces one that gazed on him with pity, and to her he gave an image of his face.

May our faces be shaped by grace into tenderness and welcome, "true images" of his. When I traveled with the Bishop of Oran through the Algerian Sahara in January 2014, we were unsure how to find our way to the monastery where we wished to spend the night. We came across a man and his two sons, Muslims, who smiled upon us and offered us hospitality in their home. I remember each face with perfect clarity. It was as if in these three faces in the wilderness I met the face of God made flesh. May each of us be such a face for whoever is lost in the desert!

Seventh Station

JESUS FALLS
FOR THE SECOND TIME

W hen Jesus fell for the first time, it was understandable. He was carrying a heavy cross. Who wouldn't? But now this is carried by Simon. So when he falls again, it must be because he is utterly exhausted. He is drained of all strength.

Our macho society is tempted to look patronizingly on people who are physically weak. The strong and healthy may even have contempt for the feeble: "poor dears," as the old and sick totter along! In the summer of 2013 I developed an illness that for a short time made it difficult for me to do ordinary things. Getting dressed was a major challenge. Baths were no longer plausible since I was hardly strong enough to get out by myself, and was ashamed to ask for help. I am grateful for that experience, because when I see people who are physically weak, I have been there, and probably will be there again before long. Our Lord shared that physical weakness and blesses it.

He also embraces us in our moral weakness. When we fall for a first time, we can blame someone else. "I am not like that!" But when we fall again and again, we are confronted with our undeniable moral flabbiness. We may be tempted to use this as an excuse. "I am just a weak person. There is nothing that I can do about it," I might say as I open yet another bottle of wine or eat the third doughnut. But that is a form of despair.

Saint Paul wrote, "when I am weak, then I am strong" (2 Cor 12:10). When I am weak, I may discover that I am not alone battling against the wind and the storms. Jesus shared our weakness so that we may share his strength. At the core of each of us is the strong Son of God. In my deepest interiority, God abides, and his grace will lift me up again and again, and put courage back in my heart. Pope Francis said that morality is not "never falling down" but always getting up again.

We keep on walking. The final words of Gregory Roberts's *Shantaram*, that remarkable story of an escaped criminal who learned to be a man of peace, invite us to endure: "For this is what we do. Put one foot forward and then the other. Lift our eyes to the snarl and smile of the world once more . . . Drag our shadowed crosses into the hope of another night. Push our brave hearts into the promise of a new day . . . For so long as fate keeps us waiting, we live on. God help us. God forgive us. We live on."

Eighth Station

THE WOMEN
OF JERUSALEM

During his journey to the cross, the only people whom Jesus addresses are women: Mary, his mother, and the daughters of Jerusalem. Mary's heart is pierced by sorrow. But the women probably do not know Jesus. They are not his disciples. They are probably just fulfilling a pious duty of ritually mourning a man who has been condemned to death. They were professional mourners. In the icon, two of them do not even look at him.

Jesus says to them, "Daughters of Jerusalem, do not weep for me, but weep for yourselves and for your children. For behold, the days are coming when they will say, 'Blessed are the barren, and the wombs that never bore, and the breasts that never gave suck!' Then they will begin to say to the mountains, 'Fall on us'; and to the hills, 'Cover us.' For if they do this when the wood is green, what will happen when it is dry?" (Luke 23:28-31). Now their grief is formal and ritualistic; one day it will be profound and heartfelt.

Even in his agony Jesus feels deeply the pain that will be theirs when Jerusalem is destroyed. He is touched by people's pain in the pit of his stomach, and he enjoys their joy more than they do themselves.

Saint Paul tells the Romans, "Rejoice with those who rejoice, weep with those who weep" (Rom 12:15). But egotism muddies the purity of our responses. Our joy may be qualified by bitterness: Why did I not get to marry that beautiful rich heiress? Why wasn't my book such an amazing success? Or, thank God I have not got cancer, or the sack, or whatever. Donald Nicholl tells of a blind man who sat outside a Japanese Buddhist temple. He said that he always knew when he was in the presence of someone who was holy. When that person "expressed his gladness at another's good fortune, all you heard was gladness. When he expressed his sorrow, all you heard was sorrow."

God's promise is that he will take out our hearts of stone and give us hearts of flesh. A heart of flesh is one that shares another's joy without a hint of jealousy and another's sorrow without a tiny bit of *schadenfreude*. Unqualified joy is only possible when the ego no longer impedes a spontaneous identification with the other person and we no longer see the other person as our rival. Until then our happiness will always be insecure, keeping an eye open for competitors who will knock us off our perch. May the Lord chip off our stony hearts the thick rind of egoism that makes us dead to what others live!

Ninth Station

JESUS FALLS
FOR THE THIRD TIME

Jesus collapses, crushed. The most moving Stations of the Cross I ever took part in were in a poor barrio in Montevideo, Uruguay. At each station, people spoke of how they lived the passion of Jesus now and trusted that he was close to them. Sometimes he seemed invisible, but then so did they. Etienne Grieu, SJ, wrote, "A world dominated by competition engages in a formidable task of classification, not only of performances but also of people. Right at the bottom of the chart are those who are not efficient enough. They thus become invisible to others, as they are unable to demonstrate their usefulness in any of the various exchanges we take part in. . . . They also feel humiliated because they scarcely can have the means to say who they are or to make people notice the unique treasure they bear."

Katherine Boo describes the world of the very poorest of all, the people who live collecting rubbish in Mumbai. They are resilient, witty, inventive even, but doomed. She says of one of them, "His profession could wreck a body in a very short time. Scrapes from dumpster diving pocked and became infected. Where skin broke, maggots got in. Lice colonized hair, gangrene inched up fingers, calves swelled into tree trunks, and Abdul and his young brothers kept a running wager about which of the scavengers would be the next to die." Nearer at home in the West, people can be crushed by low wages, wondering whether to eat or keep the house warm, dependent on food banks. Often they are despised by the media. Rowan Williams and Larry Elliott note, "Media representations of chavs, feral children, obese men and women, teenage mothers and drunken brawling have been used to define working-class life."

Jesus' fall brings him close to them so that they too may one day share his glory. Oscar Romero adapted a saying of St. Irenaeus of Lyons: *Gloria Dei vivens pauper*, "The glory of God is the living poor person."

There are also those who feel crushed by moral failure, like Peter who denied Jesus three times. Jesus struggles up and carries on, one step nearer to the cross, and one step nearer to Easter. Then he will lift the burden from Peter, and from us all, with infinite delicacy. Without even referring to his failure, he will give Peter three opportunities to unspeak it: "do you love me more than these [others]?" (John 21:15). Peter will be able to reach down below that superficial desire to save his skin to the deep, abiding hunger of his life, the love of his Lord: "you know that I love you." And then he too will be able to stand up and walk again. Whatever we have done, Jesus lifts us to our feet.

Tenth Station

JESUS IS STRIPPED OF HIS GARMENTS

Jesus is stripped of all his clothes. On the cross he will be naked. Genesis tells us that when Adam and Eve ate the fruit from the tree of knowledge of good and evil, they became aware that they were naked, and they were ashamed. Why were they suddenly ashamed? Having eaten of the fruit, they look at each other with new eyes. They have each become an object in the eyes of the other person, to be assessed and judged.

We often look at people knowingly, measuring their achievements, noting their weakness. Our gaze strips them, not only in lust but also in judgment. "I have got him down to a T." We flinch before the eyes of other people as they weigh us up. We are naked even when we are clothed. Our qualities are assessed by our managers, our fellow workers. We are judged for our beauty, our sexual performance, our failures large and small. People will examine our clothes, judging our status and our income. We may fall into the hands of the media and be taken to pieces.

Even at home, we may feel judged by the eyes of people whom we most love. Jesus is close to us then, sharing our nakedness, and bearing our shame, mocked, apparently a failed Messiah. The gospels quote Psalm 22: "I can count all my bones— / they stare and gloat over me; / they divide my garments among them, / and for my raiment they cast lots" (vv. 17-18). Even the clothes of Jesus are mere booty, to be shared between the soldiers to supplement their pay. They are part of his "net value." The Son of the Most High God is treated as a piece of property, redeeming all those who are bought and sold, from footballers to sex workers. Who does not have a price?

In the film *12 Years a Slave*, we see laid bare the most brutal commodification of human beings that has ever taken place. Slaves are stripped for inspection, their muscles tested, their teeth examined as if they were horses for sale. They are dehumanized. When a woman is sold away from her children, she weeps inconsolably. But her new mistress cannot believe that such a person could really have feelings like her own: "She will soon forget her children."

Today millions of people are still reduced to slavery— domestic servants are held in bondage; people and even children are sold for sex. They too must strip and be ashamed before the judging eyes of their clients. Human flesh is turned into meat. Jesus shares their humiliation.

But with the eyes of faith, we can see his nakedness otherwise. David stripped to fight Goliath. Jesus, the Son of David, strips to fight against every humiliation that we endure, every shame that makes us shrink. He climbs the cross to win the victory for our dignity.

Eleventh Station

JESUS IS NAILED TO THE CROSS

"And when they came to the place which is called The Skull, there they crucified him, and the criminals, one on the right and one on the left" (Luke 23:33). For those who loved Jesus or admired him, this must have seemed like an unbearable failure. He had so much promise: brilliance, an open heart, a healing touch, an eloquence that turned people's lives upside down. Once everything seemed possible for him. Now he was brought to the death of a criminal, hanging between two thieves. "But we had hoped that he was the one to redeem Israel," the disciples on the road to Emmaus say (Luke 24:21).

He seems to be a helpless victim, pushed around, mocked, forced to walk to the place of crucifixion, and now nailed to the cross. And yet, especially in John's gospel, he is quietly in charge. Colin Carr, OP, wrote,

"He knows what is going to happen; the people who come to arrest him are more frightened of him than he is of them. The guard who slaps him for speaking too boldly to the High Priest is given a neat put-down. When Pilate 'tries' Jesus it is more like Pilate being on trial. . . . He thirsts, not as a victim but as one who is fulfilling the scripture; his actual death is an accomplishment."

Shortly before the drama of his death begins, he says, "Now is my soul troubled. And what shall I say? 'Father, save me from this hour'? No, for this purpose I have come to this hour. Father, glorify [your] name" (John 12:27-28). He deliberately draws close to us in our helplessness. He is inside all our experiences of being lost and astray, so that we may not be victims but victors with him.

He was nailed to the cross, nailed firmly to all our failures, identified with everyone who seems to be a letdown, the child who disappoints a parent, the husband or wife who turned out to have feet of clay, the disgraced priest. He embraces all those who feel that God has abandoned them. His strong grace is in all who feel that their lives are coming apart, and that there is nothing they can do. In him, no life is a dead end. No one is ultimately a helpless victim. Our destiny is, after all, in our hands since he holds them.

Pope Benedict said, "Let us nail ourselves to him, resisting the temptation to stand apart, or to join others in mocking him." His arms are stretched open on the cross, open for everyone, showing us the height and depth, the width and breadth of God's love, which has no boundaries. This darkest moment, when the sun and the moon do not shine, is a revelation of glory.

JESUS DIES
ON THE CROSS

What can we say of anyone's death, since we do not know what it is to be dead? Dying we know, but not death. What possible words can we have for the death of God? The Word of God is silenced. What words do we have? Yet this dead man on the cross is the Word that speaks most loudly of a love beyond imagination.

The gospels describe Jesus' death differently. None of them captures the mystery entirely, but they come toward it from different angles, triangulate it, and give insights that converge in a truth beyond our grasp. Matthew and Mark show us a man who endures ever more radical abandonment. He is betrayed by Judas, denied by Peter; his chosen disciples flee from him. And then on the cross it seems that even his beloved Father has let him down too: "My God, my God, why [have you] forsaken me?" (Matt 27:46; Mark 15:34). His beloved Abba has become a mere formal "Eloi." He is alone.

Pain and destitution often make people feel deeply alone and isolated. No one can understand the suffering that we endure. It is beyond sharing. I once visited a prison where the prisoners had been forbidden to wear the Dominican cross, which they so loved. One of them told me that he had been threatened with solitary confinement if he wore it. How ironic: solitude for wearing the emblem of the one who bore our loneliness and isolation, so that we might know that in Christ one is never alone.

In him God embraces everyone who feels abandoned and betrayed: people struggling with the loss of those whom they love, those who are angry at senseless terminal illness, those who feel that God has let them down. In Jesus, God embraces the absence of God.

The temple veil curtained off the holy of holies. It was moved only once a year to admit the high priest on the Day of Atonement. Now this curtain is ripped in two. There is no barrier between God and humanity. God has come near to us in our desolation, and so we can come into his presence.

This image of abandonment in death in Matthew and Mark is in contrast with Jesus' enthronement in glory in John. In Luke he entrusts himself to the Father, having opened the way to heaven for the good thief. He has accomplished his task. He breathes his last. He has run the course.

He throws himself into the hands of his father: "Father, into [your] hands I commit my spirit!" (Luke 23:46).

At his mother's funeral, a friend of mine, Gilbert Markus, described his son's leap of trust as an image of faith: "When Dominic was about four years old, when I took him to nursery, he would climb on top of a wall that was about one foot high at one end, and six feet high at the other. He climbed on at the low end and ran along the flat top of the wall at top speed, launching himself into the air over my head, hoping that I would catch him. I said to my mother that this seemed like a good way to live and die—to run and run, and then to leap, in the trust that a Father's hands would catch us."

Thirteenth Station

JESUS IS TAKEN DOWN FROM THE CROSS

The soldiers take down the bodies of Jesus and the thieves "in order to prevent the bodies from remaining on the cross on the Sabbath . . . the Jews asked Pilate that their legs might be broken, and that they might be taken away" (John 19:31).

The Lamb of God, not one of whose bones have been broken, has become an obstacle to the celebration of the feast. He is in the way of religion. Dictatorships and tyrannies often find Jesus inconvenient. Oscar Romero had to be disposed of because he opposed the religion of the government of El Salvador: national security. We may also sometimes find Jesus gets in the way, with his demands for nonviolence, his identification with sinners and the poor. It is tempting to celebrate our comforting religion without the disturbance of its Lord. Stanley Hauerwas wrote a prayer for the

Chapel at Duke University: "Zealous God, we confess, like your people Israel, that we tire of being 'the chosen.' Could you not just leave us alone every once in a while? Sometimes this 'Christian stuff' gets a bit much."

The soldiers want him out of the way as soon as possible, and so he is lowered to the ground to be held by his mother. In the beginning she held him as a baby. Then he was light, but now he is heavy, a dead weight that has to be lowered by pulleys and ropes, steadied by many hands. As a baby he not only weighed little, but was not burdened with a past. Now he is heavy for his mother to hold, with the burden of so much suffering, of humiliation and sorrow. Parents, like Mary, often carry the burdens of their living children: disappointed love, failed careers, unrealized hopes. It is the weight of love.

Mary holds her dead child tenderly. He is past feeling but this tenderness is right. It is his body. We are gentle with the bodies of those whom we love. They are not just bags of flesh that our soul uses for a while before escaping. This tenderness points to our deepest hope, which is not that a soul should shimmer off to heaven, but that we may rise, fully human. We may have no idea now what this can mean, and yet that is the Christian hope.

We must not wait to show our gentleness until someone is dead. Be tender while it can be felt and reciprocated. Say the word of love or gratitude while it can be heard. I saw my father the day before he died. As I left the room with my mother, I felt his glance upon me and wondered whether there was something more he wanted to say. But we were already late and I thought, "He can say it tomorrow." But the next day was too late.

Do not wait. Before the Last Supper a woman anointed Jesus. The disciples protested. But Jesus said, "She has done a beautiful thing to me. For you always have the poor with you, . . . but you will not always have me. She has done what she could; she has anointed my body beforehand for burying" (Mark 14:6-8). When the women come to the tomb to anoint Jesus, it is already too late. *Carpe diem*; grab the moment to show your love.

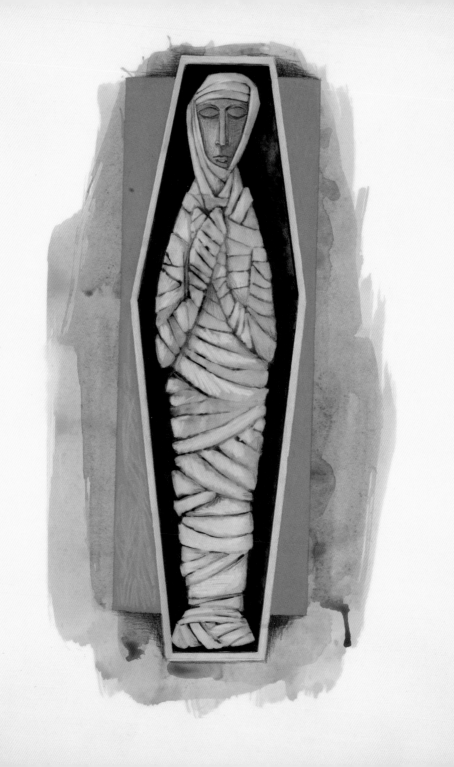

Fourteenth Station

JESUS IS PLACED
IN THE TOMB

" Joseph took the body, and wrapped it in a clean linen shroud, and laid it in his own new tomb, which he had hewn in the rock; and he rolled a great stone to the door of the tomb, and departed" (Matt 27:59-60).

This looks like the end of the story. It has come to a dead end. Nothing more is expected. A great lump of rock sits there like a giant period. The women watch as he disappears from their sight and from their lives.

He has been wrapped tightly in his burial clothes, just as his mother had wrapped him in swaddling clothes when he was a baby (Luke 2:7). Then the future seemed full of promise, as it does with most babies. Now, when he is still young, his future is quenched, and his mother once again wraps him tightly in clothes. In a poem by George Mackay Brown, the Good Thief watches Jesus being prepared for burial by his mother, and prays,

> That the hands of such a woman
> Fold me gravewards.
> Bear me and all men in her folds of light.

It looks like an end, but he is on the cusp of a new beginning. There lies before him an unimaginable future, which he will share with everyone whose life seems to have reached a final impasse. No dead end can finally defeat God's creative touch.

The African-American spiritual asks, "Were you there when they laid him in the tomb?" We were all there, every one of us, when we feared that there was no way forward, when the path was blocked by some great rock. He is there whenever we feel entombed, hemmed in, in the darkness.

"And on the seventh day God finished his work which he had done, and he rested on the seventh day from all his work which he had done. So God blessed the seventh day and hallowed it, because on it God rested from all his work which he had done in creation" (Gen 2:2-3). On the cross Jesus finishes all the work that he must do: "It is finished" (John 19:30). Now he rests. Saint Ambrose of Milan wrote, "The sixth day is now completed; the sum of the work of the world has been concluded. . . . Surely it is time now for us to make our contribution of silence, for now God rests from his work of making the world."

Jesus said, "Truly, truly, I say to you, unless a grain of wheat falls into the earth and dies, it remains alone; but if it dies, it bears much fruit" (John 12:24). Now the seed is buried in the soil. All that we can do is await the gift of its fecundity. "Tomorrow the Son of Man will walk in a garden / Through drifts of apple-blossom" (George Mackay Brown).

I once visited the tomb of Bishop Pierre Claverie in Oran, Algeria. He was murdered in 1996 for his opposition to violence and because he promoted friendship between Muslims and Christians. His tomb has become a place of pilgrimage for Christians and Muslims alike. On it are often placed flowers. God's grace brings springtime for every one of us.

REFERENCES

Preface

Gregory of Nyssa, *Epist.* 2.16-17.

Martin Luther, quoted in Robert Lerner, review of *The Sepulchre of Christ and the Medieval West*, by Colin Morris, *Times Literary Supplement* (August 19, 2005).

Jerome, *Epist.* 46.5, quoted in Pierre Maraval, "The Earliest Phase of Christian Pilgrimage in the Near East (Before the Seventh Century)," Dumbarton Oaks Papers, no. 56 (2002).

Fourth Station: Jesus Is Met by His Blessed Mother

Robert Burns, "A Mother's Lament for the Death of Her Son" (1838).

Seamus Heaney, "Seeing Things," in *Opened Ground: Selected Poems 1966–1996* (New York: Farrar, Straus & Giroux, 1998), 20.

Gravity, directed by Alfonso Cuarón, Warner Bros., 2013.

Fifth Station: Simon of Cyrene Helps Jesus to Carry His Cross

Catherine of Siena, *Catherine of Siena: The Dialogue*, trans. Suzanne Noffke, OP (New York: Mahwah, 1980), 38.

Sixth Station: Veronica Wipes the Face of Jesus

Graham Greene, *Monsignor Quixote* (New York: Simon & Schuster, 1982), 115.

Pope Francis, "A Big Heart Open to God: The Exclusive Interview with Pope Francis," by Antonio Spadaro, SJ, *America*, September 30, 2013, http://www.americamagazine.org/pope-interview.

Marilynne Robinson, *Gilead* (New York: Farrar, Straus & Giroux, 2004), 66.

Seventh Station: Jesus Falls for the Second Time

Paul Vallely, *Pope Francis: Untying the Knots* (London: Bloomsbury, 2013), 147.

Gregory David Roberts, *Shantaram* (New York: St. Martin's Press, 2004), 933.

Eighth Station: The Women of Jerusalem

Donald Nicholl, *Holiness* (New York: Seabury Press, 1981), 89.

Ninth Station: Jesus Falls for the Third Time

Etienne Grieu, SJ, "Discovering Who God Is in Caritas," in *Caritas: Love Received and Given*, ed. Óscar Cardinal Rodríguez Maradiaga (Rome, 2011), 18.

Katherine Boo, *Behind the Beautiful Forevers: Life, Death, and Hope in a Mumbai Undercity* (New York: Random House, 2012), 35.

Rowan Williams and Larry Elliott, *Crisis and Recovery: Ethics, Economics and Justice* (New York: Palgrave Macmillan, 2010), 62.

Tenth Station: Jesus Is Stripped of His Garments

12 Years a Slave, directed by Steve McQueen, Regency Enterprises, 2013.

Eleventh Station: Jesus Is Nailed to the Cross

Colin Carr, OP, "In Charge of His Helplessness," Good Friday sermon, http://torch.op.org/preaching_sermon_item .php?sermon=5735.

Cardinal Joseph Ratzinger, Office for the Liturgical Celebrations of the Supreme Pontiff, Way of the Cross at the Colosseum, Good Friday 2005.

Thirteenth Station: Jesus Is Taken Down from the Cross

Stanley Hauerwas, *Prayers Plainly Spoken* (Downers Grove, IL: InterVarsity Press, 1999), 26.

Fourteenth Station: Jesus Is Placed in the Tomb

George Mackay Brown, "Stations of the Cross: The Good Thief," *Following a Lark* (London: John Murray, 1996).

Ambrose of Milan, *Hexameron, Paradise, and Cain and Abel*, trans. John J. Savage, Fathers of the Church, vol. 42 (Washington, DC: Catholic University of America Press, 1961), 282.

George Mackay Brown, "The Harrowing of Hell," *Northern Lights* (London: John Murray, 1999).